Have You Ever Heard a Whale Exhale?

Story by Caroline Woodward
Art by Claire Victoria Watson

Pownal Street Press

pownal
street
press

pownalstreetpress.com

Have You Ever Heard a Whale Exhale? • ISBN 978-1-998129-07-2

Text copyright © 2024 by Caroline Woodward. Illustrations copyright © 2024 by Claire Victoria Watson. All rights reserved.

Edited by Mo Duffy Cobb. Interior designed by Jordan Beaulieu. The text was set in HVD Bodedo.

Cataloguing data available from Library and Archives Canada.

The use of any part of this publication reproduced, transmitted in any form or by any means, electronic, mechanical, photocopying, recording, or otherwise is not permitted without the prior written consent of the publisher. Requests for permission to make copies of any part of the work should be emailed to hello@pownalstreetpress.com

Our books may be purchased for promotional, educational, or business use. Please contact your local bookseller or Pownal Street Press at hello@pownalstreetpress.com to purchase.

Pownal Street Press gratefully acknowledges Mi'kma'ki, the ancestral and unceded territory of the Mi'kmaq First Nation on whose land our office is located.

Printed and bound in Canada by Friesens.

28 27 26 25 24 1 2 3 4 5

May we protect our oceans for all
children everywhere to enjoy.

Have you ever heard a whale exhale
and SLAP the water with its tail?
Breathing in after breathing out,
heaving WHOOSH with a mighty spout!

Have you ever seen a seal spy-hop,

then dive underwater with a playful plop?

Have you ever danced with an octopus?

No, but ask your friends—we will need more of us!

Have you ever smelled a big sea lion herd?
Oh my, they need a bath, on this you have my word!

Very yummy on a seaweed plate to go!

Have you ever felt the freezing north wind blow, while icy rain sprays on all of us below?

Have you ever sat upon a sun-warmed rock, where you and your friends would go to talk?

Have you ever wondered why eagles love to fly,

Have you ever thanked a falling star?

For all the things that make YOU who you are?

Caroline Woodward lived and worked at lighthouses on the West Coast of British Columbia for many years. From rocky shores or while paddling her kayak, she loves watching sea creatures and birds of all shapes and sizes. Caroline writes books for children, teens and adults including *Light Years: Memoir of a Modern Lighthouse Keeper* (Harbour: 2015). www.carolinewoodward.ca

Claire Victoria Watson was raised in Victoria, British Columbia, and spent most of her time outdoors on the ocean or in the forests. As a visual artist, her mediums of choice are pen and ink, watercolour, acrylic and digital. She is known for her stylized line work, organic colour palette, and for capturing the unique personality of the West Coast in the wildlife and ocean landscapes. Claire works as an artist, illustrator and graphic designer and enjoys a relatively minimalist, nomadic and creative lifestyle. After raising her family in Tofino and on Gabriola Island, Claire now again calls Victoria home. www.clairevictoria.art